THE BOY CHILD IS DYING

THE BOY CHILD
IS DYING

A South African Experience

Judy Boppell Peace

1817

Harper & Row, Publishers, San Francisco

Cambridge, Hagerstown, New York, Philadelphia, Washington
London, Mexico City, São Paulo, Singapore, Sydney

This is an expanded edition of a paperback book previously published by InterVarsity Press.

Harper & Row
FIRST EDITION

Library of Congress Cataloging in Publication Data

Peace, Judy Boppell.
    The boy child is dying.

    "Expanded edition of a paperback book previously published by Intervarsity Press"—Verso of CIP t.p.
    1. Peace, Judy Boppell. 2. Americans—South Africa—Biography.
3. South Africa—Race relations—Anecdotes, facetiae, satire, etc.
I. Title.
DT763.P39   1986   986.06   85–45722
ISBN 0-06-066482-7

86 87 88 89 90 HC 10 9 8 7 6 5 4 3 2 1

For Abiel and Jeminah
  who suffer because they are black

For John and Jenny
  who suffer because they are white
  and see

Foreword

These stories of South Africa evoke diverse emotions, of anger, frustration, shame, love. One feels anger that such things should happen to human beings, not because they are dishonest or wicked, but because they are black. One feels frustration because the pace of change is so slow, not only the change of law and custom, but the change of heart—and that means the white heart of course. One feels shame—if one is white—that these things are done in one's name, by one's white Parliament (because our Parliament is all white), that one is a member of the ruling class, whether one wants it or not.

Why should the emotion of love be aroused, but with tears, not joy? In one of the stories Judy Peace tells of the release of twenty-two persons who were "banned," that is, silenced and forbidden to take any part in public life, even forbidden to attend any gathering, even of friends. Most of them had been pacifists before they were banned; now many of them had come to believe that change would come about only by violence.

Judy Peace reflected on the trial of the twenty-two as she sat waiting in the car, and when her black friend Mrs. Ntonsheni rejoined her, she said, "You have been crying." "Yes," Judy answered. "I have been feeling the pain of loving this land."

That pain is felt by many of us. This great and beautiful land of plain and mountain and sky, of desert and grassland, of wild flowers innumerable that at times can carpet the plain as far as the eye can see, is a land of pain also. Many visitors from many countries come to see me, and many of them say, "Ah, but your country is beautiful," and in their eyes is that look of love and pain that says as plainly as any words, "But why does it have to be what it is?" And that means of course, why do people treat people as they do? And that means, why do white people treat black people as they do? Why do they treat them as things? Why . . . and why . . . and why?

The Boy Child is Dying tells stories of love and pain, but they are not exaggerated or propagandist. They are painful because they are true, and they will give to people living in other countries a better understanding of our condition in South Africa. That is after all what the writer has tried to do, and in my view she has been eminently successful. Her style is simple and unadorned. Her stories have the ring of truth.

Alan Paton
Hillcrest, Natal, South Africa
April 1978

Preface

My husband, my children and I lived and worked in South Africa for eight years. We grew to know and love many people of black and white descent. We became aware of the tragedy for both the oppressed and the oppressor living in a virtual police state—both sides imprisoned by fear and ignorance.

The stories I have written here are all true. They all happened to me. But you can live in South Africa all your life and not really see what is happening around you. You can have eyes to see and yet not see. I have white South African friends, for example, who will read this and say these things are impossible or, "This is just our way of life, different from yours." I have other white South African friends who know these stories in many shapes and forms. They share the suffering of their land.

When we were leaving South Africa to return to the United States, a black friend said to me, "Judy, if you can help people in America to understand a little of the suffering we experience every day of our lives as black South Africans, your time here will have been worthwhile."

My hope in writing these sketches is that a few more people will have a compassionate understanding of that suffering and that this will lead to redemptive action. They are not meant to point a finger at South Africa as the most terrible of nations. A black American assured me he could write similar stories of his life in the United States. And I have friends who have been discriminated against in African countries because they were white. These stories are about South Africa simply because that is where these events took place.

Most of the names have been changed to protect people's privacy. The conversations are as I remember them. Not having an infallible memory, I trust they remain true to the spirit, if not the letter, of the words that were spoken.

PART ONE

1

She stopped speaking, looked at me and said, "Yes, I'll work for you."

Startled, I realized who had been interviewing whom. She had been introduced to me as Esther. "What is your last name?" I asked.

"Why do you want to know?'" she responded.

"Simply because I am twenty-five years old, you are at least fifty and I would feel very uncomfortable having you call me Mrs. Peace while I called you Esther."

"I am Mrs. Esther Ntonsheni." She paused. "Mrs. Peace, I worked for a woman for ten years and she never knew I had any other name than Esther."

We had been in the apartment for a month. Having someone help me with my housework was not easy. I had always done my own work. I felt guilty watching someone else do it. Dick and I had decided that, for us, not having help was irresponsible. South Africa has something called "job reservation." Though this is breaking down slowly, for the majority of the black population it means finding a job is very difficult. And working as a house servant is still one of the easiest jobs to find. Since so many people need work, we reasoned, the least we could do was hire someone to help us.

We knew the "normal" working conditions. We had

been told twelve rand (around seventeen dollars) a month was a good starting salary. Most people expected their servants to arrive around 7:30 A.M. and leave by 6:00 P.M., if they didn't live in. Servants considered themselves lucky to get an afternoon off a week. Many people felt they were being generous to give this, as it meant "managing on their own" that afternoon. We decided to ask Mrs. Ntonsheni to work a five-day week, from nine to five, with a salary above the norm. Perhaps this was one way of showing people around us new working possibilities.

Mrs. Ntonsheni entered the room. "Mrs. Peace, are you unhappy with my work?"

"No. Why do you ask?"

"Well, you are always doing it for me. I would prefer it if you left it to me!"

"I had not been sure how much to expect you to do, and I didn't want to overwork you," I replied, feeling slightly defensive.

"You are paying me a fair wage, giving me good hours and I want to feel I am earning my salary!"

Mrs. Ntonsheni took over the housework.

It wasn't more than three weeks later that Mrs. Ntonsheni said, "Mrs. Peace." I had come to recognize the tone. She had something to say. It was going to be difficult for her. She sounded defensive. "What have I done now?" I thought.

"Mrs. Peace, I have worked for white women many years—more than twenty. I was taught as a girl how to be in a white house. All the madams, they tell me I am a good servant. I do all I was taught for you. I think you don't like it. Why?"

I took a deep breath. I am not known for hiding my feelings and I too had been frustrated by our relationship. She was right. She had played the role of perfect servant, always "happy," constantly ready to please us. We could not have asked for more from a servant, and I assured her of this. "You do your job wonderfully well, Mrs. Ntonsheni. I couldn't ask for a better servant. Every morning, you are here punctually. 'I am fine,' you answer in response to my greeting. Your life is always fine. Yet I see traces of worry in your eyes. I see signs of suffering. I know your life cannot always be fine. You work hard, too hard. It is impossible to get you to rest. You feel guilty just sitting and relaxing for a few minutes. When I enter the room, you seem tense and I feel it is kinder to keep out of your way. Mrs. Ntonsheni, I didn't hire you to be a servant under me. I hired another human being to help me with my work. I don't feel comfortable in the master/servant role. I'd like us to work at relating as two women—equals. I'm beginning to understand a little how hard that will be for you, but I'd like to try."

A few days later Mrs. Ntonsheni shouted from the kitchen, "Mrs. Peace, are you busy?"

"Not very. Why?"

"Well, I'm ironing and it is starting to rain and there are clothes on the line." A long pause.

"I'll get them," I said, as I left my letters and went out the back door, grabbing the clothes basket from the kitchen corner on the way.

"Whew, that rain is really coming down." I stamped my feet, shook my hair and plopped down the basket. Mrs. Ntonsheni gave me a long, searching look. It was no light thing she had done. I appreciated the risk she had taken and the beginning of trust it showed.

"Thank you," I said.

She nodded and I left the room.

2

We were guests for a week in the home of kind, generous people. One evening I was making some punch for dinner. Gloria, the servant, was watching.

"It looks good," she said.

"Here, try some," I said.

"She can't have that!" Linda, the daughter of the household, objected.

"I made it and I'd like to give her some."

Silence, a bewildered look, then: "If she must have some, she can't drink out of *our* cups, she will have to go to her room out back and get her own tin cup!"

"That seems rather silly when there are plenty of cups here," I said as I handed Gloria a cup of juice.

No mistaking the look of fear in Gloria's face. But as we looked at one another, her face broke into a half smile and she drank the juice. Linda looked unhappy, ashamed, confused, not knowing why Gloria shouldn't drink out of their cups.

3

William was puttering around the garden. He had "a room" at the back of the property, provided by the landlord as part of his pay for keeping up the yard. I suspect his quality of work was in direct proportion to his estimation of his own value as a person, which wasn't very high. He glanced sideways at me as I sauntered up.

"My wife may be coming to stay tomorrow. Her time is near for the baby to come and I want her close to me and to a hospital. Do you mind?"

William was asking much more than if we minded. It is against South African law for a black man and woman to live as man and wife in a "white area." They might begin to believe they belonged there. The police raided servants' quarters periodically to be sure no "illegal natives" were on the premises. If a man's wife was found with him, she could go to jail and the occupants of the "white house" could be fined fifty rand for "harboring people unnecessary to the area."

"William, I'm glad she is coming. We will help watch out for her."

One night, not long afterwards, Dick and I were awakened by a sharp, insistent knock. William stood wringing his hands. Victoria, down on her hands and knees, was wild-eyed, frantic with pain.

"Get her on the bed," said Dick. "I'll call the ambulance."

He and William, feeling their part of the job was over, disappeared into the living room.

Victoria was beyond reason. She grabbed me around the neck and seemed quite capable of strangling me.

"Victoria, let go and listen to me,'" I shouted. I had just had our first child by natural childbirth so the method was familiar to me. "I can show you a way to breathe that will help the pain. You can control yourself and make this a lot easier!"

We both felt desperate enough to try anything and before long she was huffing and puffing regularly.

The baby arrived as the ambulance pulled up. We were greatly relieved, for the baby was born still encased in the sack and neither Victoria nor I was sure of what to do.

"Thank God you're here," I said to the two white men at the door. "The baby has been born, but something is wrong. We need your help."

"If the baby is born, we'll be leaving, lady. Our orders were just to pick up a woman in labor!"

"Do you know how to save that baby?" I asked.

"That's not the question, lady. You see, legally, we were called to take a black woman in labor to the hospital and—"

"I don't care about legalities. If you don't get in there and help that baby, I'll have it in every paper in South Africa and America that you two are murderers." This I said very quietly, as I blocked the door with my arm.

Once the baby was out of danger, the men agreed to take Victoria and the baby to the hospital where the cord would be cut, as they did not see this as their responsibility. I wrapped the baby up for protection against the night air. The men refused to touch her once they had dealt with the sack. As they carried the stretcher out, one of the men turned to me and said, "You must be new to this country, lady. Your attitudes will change!"

I sat deep in thought for a long time after they left. It was hard for me to believe what had just happened. I think I had always felt it was instinctive to save a baby's life if you could, but these men *had not wanted to*.

Late in the morning I answered a knock at the door to find Victoria standing there with her baby.

"What are you doing here?" I asked.

"The hospital was too crowded. I was lying on the floor in the hall. I was hungry and no one had fed me, so I walked home," she said. The black hospital was about a half-hour's drive from our house.

As I was fixing lunch, I glanced out the window. Victoria was filling a bucket at the water faucet. I rushed out to the back yard.

"Victoria, you shouldn't be carrying a heavy bucket. Why don't you get William to do it for you?"

"He is busy, and this is woman's work. I need the water to wash myself and the child. The baby needs water to drink too."

I felt a twinge of guilt that it had not occurred to Victoria to ask me for help.

"You should get help. You could hurt yourself carrying heavy loads now."

Victoria shrugged, shifted the bucket and pushed the door open with her shoulder.

"One does what one must."

A year later I again opened the door to discover Victoria standing there. She had come to show us Tandi, a beautiful, bright one year old.

"Victoria, she is so bright," I said.

"Yes, isn't that a shame," she replied. Victoria knew that to grow up bright and black in South Africa is to live a life of perpetual pain and frustration.

4

Benjamin made a face as he put down the cup.

"Judy, I am truly glad I tried Turkish coffee tonight. Now I never have to drink it again in my entire life!"

The laughter rose and fell. We all settled comfortably into our armchairs.

"Benjamin, you must bring Rachel with you next time you come. I'm looking forward to getting to know her."

A flicker of pain crossed his face. "She won't come, Judy."

"Why not?"

"She is afraid."

"Of me?"

"Yes, of you and all you stand for. She has never related to a white woman in any role other than master/servant."

"*You* are not afraid. Why?"

"I grew up in Lesotho and have had white friends. I have chosen to work with white men in South Africa in the hope of helping bring about change. But it is very hard, even for me."

"Benjamin, what can I do? You and Dick work together. You tell people love can conquer all barriers. Yet you say your wife is afraid to enter my house as a guest. This makes a mockery of your own hope. Rachel and I must meet."

Benjamin's furrowed brow indicated concentrated thought. "Judy, you must begin where Rachel is and she is afraid to enter your home as your equal. She wants to improve her English. Perhaps if you could work with her in a teacher/student role, it would give her more security in meeting you. It would be up to you to make it into something more."

Within a week, Rachel arrived for English lessons. We solemnly opened the grammar book and began. Her English was poor and progress slow.

"Rachel, would you like some lunch?" I asked, when we had been studying sentences along enough.

"Please don't bother, Mrs. Peace."

"Rachel, if you call me Mrs. Peace one more time, I shall be forced to begin calling you Mrs. Mthsali. Both of us being around twenty-six years old, that seems silly!"

The words were wrenched out against the will—"All right . . . Judy."

I left her to go and prepare lunch. A few minutes later Mrs. Ntonsheni entered the kitchen. Looking up, I asked what was wrong.

"Rachel is terrified of eating lunch with you, Mrs. Peace. She asked me to get her out of it. I told her not to be afraid, that you won't bite."

Two years later, we were staying in Johannesburg. Dick's work had taken us there for a year. Benjamin and Rachel were having dinner with us. They too were in the city of gold. We were discussing Mrs. Ntonsheni's relatives.

"They all want to see Mrs. Ntonsheni while she is here, so I suggested she have them over for dinner," I said. "Dick and I made arrangements to be out that afternoon, as Mrs. Ntonsheni felt they wouldn't come if they knew we would be home. She said they would be afraid of eating with us."

Rachel looked at me. "I know how they feel," she said.

5

South Africa is lovely beyond description: open veld, rolling hills, grand mountains, rugged coastline, flowers and foliage beautiful to behold. To explore and experience the sheer lushness and infinite variety of the land is pure pleasure. We spent delightful days trekking through game reserves, canoeing down quiet rivers, climbing mountain trails, searching out bushman paintings and hidden springs. The beaches of South Africa are some of the finest in the world, miles of white glistening sand bordering the warm waters of the Indian Ocean and the harsher waters of the Atlantic. Here are places to relax and be refreshed.

"Mrs. Ntonsheni, would you like to go to the beach with us this Saturday?"

Eyes sparkle. "I've never seen the ocean. Yes, I'd like to go."

"You have lived forty miles from the ocean most of your life and have never seen it?"

"Never had a way to get there." Her eyes slowly dulled. "I can't go with you," she said. "For a moment I forgot."

"Why not?"

"I'm not allowed on the white beaches. You would have to drive ten miles out to the 'non-European beach' and leave me there. I wouldn't enjoy being alone in a strange place. I would be allowed to stay with you on the white beach as a nanny to the children, but people would stare at me. I would feel uncomfortable. I wouldn't be allowed to put my feet in the water either. No, it is impossible for me to come with you."

Saturday came and we went to the sea. The relaxing warmth of sun on sand felt uncomfortably hot that day. The simple pleasure of play on the beach had become an escape from the harsh realities of a sick society, a place for the ostrich to stick his head in the sand.

The dinner was good, the company pleasant. We took our after-dinner coffee to the garden, loath to miss the last light of the warm summer sun. One of the men was speaking.

"Heard a story the other day that illustrates perfectly

the lack of intelligence of our Kaffirs. Seems there were three boys who thought it was time they each owned a suit. One of those boys made a decent wage; the second was working part-time; the third had no job. The first month the two working boys pooled their money and bought a suit for their friend out of work. The second month they bought a suit for the part-time worker. The third month they bought a suit for the full-time worker. Now any man with a slight bit of brain should have figured out that if he were making the most money, he would be far ahead just buying a suit for himself!"

Laughter . . . the gentle laughter of a fond parent amused at the antics of a child.

It was the Christmas season. Sarah, a friend and frequent visitor, had dropped in for tea. Sarah, Mrs. Ntonsheni used to say, did not act as if she had been raised in white South Africa. The two had become friends.

"Mrs. Ntonsheni, what do you want for Christmas this year?" Sarah asked.

"Sugar."

There was a twenty-five pound bag of sugar in the car when I drove Mrs. Ntonsheni home for Christmas weekend. When she returned, we talked about the festivities we had enjoyed with our families.

Mrs. Ntonsheni turned to Sarah. "We all enjoyed the sugar. It made the Christmas meals nicer."

"What do you mean, 'enjoyed,'" I asked. "You couldn't have finished that bag in three days."

"We gave a cup each to the people who live around us. It is gone now."

"That sugar could have lasted you for months, Mrs.

Ntonsheni. Now you have none. Why did you give it all away?"

"We couldn't have enjoyed sugar for Christmas if we had hoarded it, knowing our neighbors had none, could we?"

7

She swung through the gate in a hurry. In her preoccupation, she left it open. There was no mistaking the fear. Its single, overriding power had blocked out all other sensations. The fear was focused with fanatical narrowmindedness on the inert bundle in the girl's arms.

Mrs. Ntonsheni dropped the cup back into the soapy water as she heard the sharp cry from the yard. When she returned to the house, she brought the fear with her. It was catching.

"It's the baby, Mrs. Peace. I told her not to take him to the witch doctor. She says his cough was worse today. She had no money for the hospital and the hospital is slow and she would wait most of the day for help. The witch doctor lets you pay him later when you have some money. The hospital wants the money now, before you see the doctor. But I told her not to take her son to the witch doctor. The witch doctor is sometimes good, sometimes bad. Now my grandson is very bad. He looks very bad. My baby, my beautiful baby boy!" Her voice rose and fell, rose and fell and finally broke into the wail that the words had been holding back.

Dick had left his study to investigate when he too heard the cry from the yard. He entered the kitchen now, pale and worried.

"We must get the child to the hospital at once," he said. "His condition is critical."

In that moment we felt helpless and angry before the stupidity of apartheid. The white hospital is within five minutes of our door. The black hospital is a half-hour drive. The white hospital will not accept blacks under any circumstances.

The child, the mother, Mrs. Ntonsheni and Dick piled into the car. The sounds of gears forced into reverse, running feet, the creaking of the gate opening wide, rubber against gravel as the car backed up: the journey began.

How long is a half-hour? Long enough to listen for a heartbeat that gets fainter and fainter, long enough to feel the dear hot chubby hand go limper and limper, long enough to wipe over and over again the beads of perspiration from the smooth brown forehead and the thick curly black hair, and more than long enough to look into the once bright eyes—large brown beautiful eyes—that friends were always exclaiming over—eyes that grow dull and disinterested as the car speeds over the concrete. A half-hour can be a very long time.

Dick let out the women and the child at the emergency exit and parked the car. When he entered the hospital, he found them at the end of a long line winding down a corridor.

"Why didn't you go to the front of the line? The baby cannot wait."

"We did," said Mrs. Ntonsheni. "We told the man our

child is very sick, we need help now. He said all these people wait for hours. We wait too."

Dick felt the anger again, but not the helplessness. He marched them up to the man guarding the door. Inside was the overworked doctor.

"Look at this child," he said to the man. "You can see his condition. This baby is dying! If he waits at the end of the line, it will be too late! The child is dying, don't you understand?"

The man set his chair on all four legs, looked from one face to the other, hesitated, shrugged and let them pass. Dick's white skin had won.

As they entered the room, they said to the doctor, "We have a baby, a boy child, who is dying."

The boy child was not dying. The boy child was dead.

We pulled into the drive-in restaurant. We stopped at one as often as possible when Mrs. Ntonsheni was in the car. We could not go into a restaurant together—one of the inconveniences of "petty apartheid." We ordered and settled back to wait, grateful for the chance to break our journey.

"Which order is for the girl?" the man at the car window asked Dick for the second time.

"Which girl do you mean? We have two daughters,"

said Dick. Jenny and Lisa romped together in the back seat oblivious to the conversation.

"You know what I mean." The man glared at us.

"No," Dick persisted politely, "I don't know what you mean."

The man took a deep breath. His face was flushed. His discomfort was evident. He pointed accusingly at Mrs. Ntonsheni.

"That girl!" There, he'd said it. He relaxed his breath and almost smiled.

"You couldn't possibly mean Mrs. Ntonsheni. She is at least fifty years old."

"You knew I meant her."

"No, I expected you to know the difference between a woman and a girl," said Dick. "My mistake."

"Which is her order," asked the man.

"What possible concern is that to you?" Dick replied.

"Natives cannot be served on our regular dishes. She has to have a tin plate and cup." The man was quick to catch the horror and disbelief that crossed our faces. "Nothing personal," he hastened to assure us. "We would lose customers if we didn't enforce this policy."

The man stood alone in the car space as the five customers he had just lost drove away.

My anger sputtered over in irrational statements and oaths against apartheid.

"Mrs. Peace, don't let yourself get so upset. You aren't hurting that man or the system or anyone but yourself. That was a minor incident for me. One of many I encounter in the course of a day. If I allowed myself to feel anger every time I was treated that way, I would be a sick woman by now."

"It was so stupid, so wrong, so humiliating," I said.

"Yes, it was."

"How can you sit back and do nothing? Don't you care if you have to live this way?"

"It is my daily prayer to see this country change. Anything that brings a good change, I am for. But useless anger, destructive violence—that hurts me more than the man who calls me girl."

Years later Dick talked with a man in Cape Town. He was a "Cape colored" who had been thrown out of his home. There was a lovely section of the Cape which had been a colored area for three generations. A community of neatly kept, colorful cottages along the coast of the Indian Ocean. The government decided it would make a nice resort for the white community. The area was reclassified as a white area. The colored people, many had lived there all their lives, were moved *en masse* to a new location: a dry, sandy spot where forty m.p.h. winds whip the sand mercilessly into eyes, nose and throat, making the soulless concrete rooms called homes seem almost havens. The new colored area is miles from Cape Town. People ride buses for an hour to get to work.

"How do you stand this," Dick asked his friend.

"The first year, I nearly went insane. I woke from the little sleep I'd get to a sense of fury, frustration, hatred. There came a morning when I didn't want to wake up. My bitterness had eaten away my desire for life. The injustice that had been dealt me and my people was beyond my capacity to endure. 'This,' I said to myself, 'is not smart. The white men are enjoying our homes. My hatred is not touching them. It only poisons me. Once I loved life, now I despise it.' I decided then that I would look at life again and accept the gifts of each day. I work all I can for the coming of a just society for my land, but I cannot afford the luxury of hating my oppressors. I think I have come to pity them instead."

9

South Africa exists to a large degree by grace of the mine workers. Without the revenue from the gold mines, the economy would grind to a halt. Every year thousands of black men leave their homes to work in the mines. The homelands are places of children, women and old men. The young men give their youth and vitality away in the dark underground caverns which yield the precious metal. When we were in South Africa, they received in return for the strength of their manhood approximately a dollar a day.

For eleven months of the year, men are herded together into dormitories "according to their tribes." The government claims they are "preserving cultural identities" in this way. It is a small coincidence that it also keeps the blacks of South Africa from feeling a strong national identity. History does continue to move forward, and that national identity is growing in spite of the government's concern for "nourishing one's tribal roots."

All manner of social problems arise from the housing situation. Picture hundreds of men sharing bunks in crowded barracks; some bunks made of concrete with no mattresses. No family life, no male-female relationships, no nurture from the earth each lived with most of his childhood. Much crime and prostitution take place, giving rise to the myth of the immoral, irresponsible black man.

"How can our natives stand to live like that? If anyone doubts the black man is different from the white, he only has to see what goes on in those mine compounds. A white man couldn't survive there!"

Jim, a friend, arrived at a suburban Johannesburg home. The hostess had provided an elegant, bountiful table for her guests. The host, a mine executive, was in an expansive mood. The evening was warm, the guests mellow, content. The host raised his glass of superb South African wine.

"A toast to South Africa, our beloved land. Where else in the world could we enjoy life as fully and live so well?"

The people smiled, nodded, clinked their glasses and looked out over the manicured, well-lighted garden.

"I would be interested in the opinions of your mine workers lying on their cold, hard bunks, as to the benefits of being a South African tonight," said Jim.

The easy silence had been broken, the evening tarnished. Jim was not invited back.

My husband and I were visiting Lesotho. A friend, a priest, invited us to spend a day in the Lesotho mountains with him.

"I will show you the necessities of life today."

We started out on horseback early in the morning. There were no roads to where we were going. We passed through fields of mealies (corn) and were lulled by the rustling of the stalks in the warm summer breeze. We shouted greetings to children at play who stood watching us pass, their noses full of mucus and their tummies full of nothing. We crossed glistening, tumbling, mountain streams. We felt heady with the grandeur of the land.

We came upon a hut set in the side of the hill. A tall, blanketed Masotho greeted us at the door and invited us to see his home. There was a small room. We saw two blankets in the corner, a mat, a large kettle, one large spoon, a knife, two plates and a suitcase.

"This is all he owns," said our priest friend. "This is all a man needs to survive. He and his family eat off the land. Mealies is their staple."

"I have just returned from a year in the mines," the Masotho offered. "I am still getting used to all this beauty and fresh air, the richness of the silence and the freedom of my own place."

"Do you like working in the mines?" I inquired.

"I hate the mines. I hate going back! A month here is never enough!"

Startled by the intensity of his reply, I asked, "Why do you go?"

"It is better than watching my children starve."

10

I looked up from breakfast as Mrs. Ntonsheni entered the room. "You were at the church last night," I said.

"Yes. How did you know?"

"You always have a special light in your eyes when you've been to church. The services must be marvelous."

"Yes, not like your white church. You always stop just as the people are beginning to warm up. We sing and dance and lose our tiredness. Last night Mrs. Kekana needed help. She needs to work to feed her children. She didn't have twenty-five cents for bus fare, so she could go to town to look for work. We all gave money until we had twenty-five cents. We had to go around the room three times to get it since it's near the end of the month! A young man talked to us and told us that we were selling out our own people by believing in Jesus, because Jesus is the white man's God. The name the white man uses to keep the black man down. I said, 'Young man, if Jesus is the white man's God, why did he heal my arm that had gone limp like a snake? I asked Jesus to please help me, because I needed my arm to work so my children could eat. When I asked Jesus to make my arm well, he did; and I am very black. Why would he help a poor black woman if he is the white man's God?' "

Mrs. Ntonsheni is a woman blessed, for she has found a sure foundation upon which to build her life, a way to walk that is true and life giving. Not all her fellow countrymen are so fortunate.

The sad truth is that for many black South Africans, the road to self-fulfillment is exceedingly hard. Too many are still victims of a cultureless world.

The following are excerpts from a letter written by a friend who farms in South Africa.

"I will tell you something of our workers. All the bachelors have left—either from drinking too much or from serious V.D. troubles. Of the seven families we have here, one father has been to school for two years and two of his five children have gone to school for eleven years. None of the other fathers or mothers have been to school at all. They cannot read or write or count beyond three. It means when Robert teaches them to drive a tractor and tries to tell them about 4th and 5th and 6th gears, they're completely out of their depth. Can you imagine parents with no education trying to cope with four, five and six children of their own? The fathers have no idea that their money is to be shared with their families. They buy clothing, radios, etc., for themselves—even beds—but not for their wives and children. We give milk every day and meat regularly, and we give the families every male calf born. But from the remarks of the mothers, one gathers that the adults, mainly the men, eat and drink all and the children see nothing. Their reasoning is that they did not have anything as children. How does one explain to people whose brains are deficient through lack of education and malnutrition that a lack of protein in childhood results in a deficient brain? The babies drink from their mothers until they are two, which is a godsend, but I've just struggled with a mother who had a breast abscess and who fed her little chap on porridge (hardly cooked) and absolutely no milk. She and her husband drank all the milk we were providing and the result was a very sick child. It's difficult, as mother and father are charming people and their errors are errors of ignorance, not cruelty.

"I've put one of the mothers, who is an alcoholic, on a daily pill which prevents her from drinking. She was drunk every day and really bad on Sundays. She was very ill, as she would spend nights outside without realizing she was there. She was also raped several times. I told her about the pill in one of her sober moments and she begged me to get it for her. I intend to keep her on this pill until she is well and enjoying the difference and then I will send her for psychological treatment. She is by far my favorite mother here—my children adore her too. She has a golden heart, a dull brain and a strong desire to live (now that she is alive again)."

11

"South Africa is made up of many different tribes and cultures. It is important to preserve the unique identity of each tribe. This is why separate homelands are vital. People of different tribes were not meant to live together. This can be illustrated in any household where servants of different tribes dwell together. The constant feuding creates disharmony."

Thus goes the South African myth. One is tempted to respond that the same feuding can be found in most any household.

In one of the homelands there is a mission hospital that is a decided embarrassment to the South African government. The people who run the place believe and act on the principle that we all belong to the human family; that while we have an inner tendency toward broken relationships, we were created to live in love with all our brothers and sisters. These people believe it is possible to choose to act in love toward one another and to learn together all this means. The journey is not always easy. There is anger, frustration, pain to deal with, yet great growth and joy and life as well.

It is heartening to see a part of the church being a source of real light in the South African situation. This is not always so. One evening Mrs. Ntonsheni went with me to an integrated religious service. The possibilities for being together at such a gathering were few, so we took advantage of this opportunity. After the service, I asked Mrs. Ntonsheni what she thought of it.

"Mrs. Peace, the man who spoke has been in your home. I never suspected by the way he treated me that he could say the good words he said tonight."

One weekend Henrietta, Jim and I went to the mission hospital. Henrietta, a black girl, worked with my husband, as did Jim. We all felt a need for a time apart on this island of sanity battered on all sides by the darkness of apartheid.

It was a beautiful weekend. We played together, ate together, walked and talked together. Wonder of wonders, Henrietta and I shared a room. Black and white are not allowed to sleep under the same roof in South Africa. It is illegal.

The husband and wife who run the hospital are both doctors, both beautiful human beings. Just watching them go through a normal day is an exhausting and an inspiring experience.

Dr. Wilson took us on his morning rounds of the hospital. Of all the wards we saw, the ward for children suffering from malnutrition made the strongest impact on me. The skeletal figures, lying listlessly in small cribs bore slight resemblance to human children. Many, hovering on the fragile border between life and death, had lost all interest in the environment surrounding them. They did not even turn their heads or move their eyes as we passed by. Others cried out in strange, terrible wails; sitting on their haunches, rocking back and forth—full of fear for their strange surroundings and full of the pain of severe malnutrition. Intravenous devices were everywhere, as many of these dear little souls were beyond the normal process of eating.

I picked up one small, sobbing stranger and rocked and cuddled him until his cries subsided. When I reluctantly returned him to his crib, he fell into a light sleep. The next child I reached out to shrunk from me and cried more hysterically. Dr. Wilson gave me a look full of understanding.

"You can't win them all, Judy. Come, we must move on."

"These children look so sick, Dr. Wilson."

"Unfortunately, some of them won't survive. These were in the last stages of starvation before they were brought to us. There is little we can do to help."

"Is there no way to get them here earlier?"

"Regrettably, our hospital has not the time or resources to practice preventative medicine. We are more like an emergency station in the midst of crisis. This small hospital serves over twelve thousand people scattered over large distances. As more people are sent back to the homelands, the number will increase. We can barely keep up with those who come to us. You have seen the waiting lines of those wanting to be admitted. Because it is difficult to get here, few people come before a problem is acute. We do get out in the district for house calls as often as possible, yet we only touch the tip of the iceberg. We cannot do all we wish, but we do all we can."

Dr. Wilson's normal day starts around 5:00 A.M. and ends well past midnight. He is a man who has reached retirement age and his mission board worries about the pace he keeps.

"They ordered me back to England for a complete check-up last year," he says, "convinced I must be on the edge of collapse. To their surprise, the tests confirmed that I am in good shape. My tests compared to a man much younger than I. I told them I also sleep like a baby."

After dinner, Dr. Wilson sometimes lectures to the nurses on relevant diseases. He lectures without notes and manages to keep the attention of young girls already tired from a day's hard work. He finished this particular evening with a good dramatic reading of *The Snow Goose*, for all who were interested.

Our weekend flew by and too soon we found ourselves heading home. After many hours of driving we realized we were hungry and pulled up to a café. We all felt the shock of re-entry, for Henrietta could not go in with us.

"Let's have a sit-in," I said.

Henrietta smiled. "I'm not the martyr type, Judy. Just go in and get the food. I'm starved."

We bought meat pies, climbed back into the car and drove off under the darkening sky.

12

It started out like any other day. Mrs. Ntonsheni was washing clothes. Rebecca was playing with the girls. I was straightening up the house. Rebecca, Mrs. Ntonsheni's niece, taught school in Lesotho. She was staying with her aunt while being treated for an ulcer at the local black hospital. For the past two months she had been coming often to spend the day, as she found staying home alone boring.

Harsh pounding on the back door interrupted our activities. Mrs. Ntonsheni entered the room, her eyes apprehensive.

"A man wants to talk to you. He is a white man that watches us. He wants to see my passbook."

The man who greeted me was pleasant, courteous. He was well built, a man used to being taken seriously, a man without humor.

"Just a routine check, madam. Is there anyone else working here, a boy perhaps, working on the house?"

"Interesting you should ask that," I said. "There was a boy fixing the roof yesterday. Today he is gone."

"Did he have a passbook?"

"Yes. We got him through the Bantu Employment Bureau. Everything was in order."

I did not tell him that David was the son of a friend's

friend. He had just come to town and was desperate to make some money, just enough to eat. We had told him to go and sit in the employment office. Dick then went and applied for someone to work on the roof. The bureau clerk suggested Dick choose from the many people sitting in the office waiting room.

"I'll take that young man," Dick said, pointing at David. It is not a simple matter to hire a black man in South Africa.

Mrs. Ntonsheni had gone to her room and was back with her passbook. All was in order. I started back to my work, having been dismissed by the Bantu Affairs man. An eruption of sound caused me to turn quickly. Rebecca was shouting and gesticulating at the black policeman who accompanied the white man. The black policeman looked surly and sounded angry. Rebecca rushed toward me.

"He says I have to go with them because I have no passbook. He got angry when I told him I was a person, not a dog." Her defiance melted into distress. "Don't let them take me. What can I do?"

I looked at the white man, standing clothed in a special calm that is peculiar to officials with authority.

"She will have to come with us," he said. "She knows the laws. She must carry her passbook at all times."

"She will not leave this house and you will not enter it," I said. "You are not a proper policeman. You have no authority to arrest this woman."

He slowly drew his wallet out of his hip pocket, thumbed methodically through his papers and handed me a card.

"The bearer of this card is authorized to arrest any suspicious Bantu. Anyone obstructing said arrest is liable to fine and/or imprisonment."

"I still demand a uniformed policeman."

"Very well, madam. Call this number."

I was told by a friendly voice that someone would come right over. I served us all cold lemonade as we waited. It was a hot day. The captain of the precinct arrived within five minutes.

"You are getting yourself in serious trouble, madam."

"Couldn't you let Rebecca bring her passbook to her office tomorrow?" I asked.

"Against the rules."

"What would happen to me if you stopped me in my car and I didn't have my license," I asked.

"We would ask you to bring it to the station within a few days."

"Exactly. So why can't Rebecca bring her passbook to the station within a few days?"

"Because, madam, she is black and you are white, and the laws are not the same for you."

"That is what I have been waiting to hear. I reject a law not based on equality. There is a higher law by which I choose to live. If Rebecca goes to jail, so do I. You cannot take her without taking me."

The awkward silence was broken by the fateful arrival of a reporter friend. Upon pulling up to our house and seeing the police car, he concluded I had gotten into some sort of crazy mess. Bob immediately addressed the police officer in Afrikaans. There was spirited conversation, sidelong glances at me and jovial laughter which dissipated the tension.

"Let me handle this," said Bob. "I will go to the police station with Rebecca and sort out the trouble, then buy these good men a beer."

Rebecca nodded her approval and I consented.

Bob was gone longer than we had expected. He returned alone. The troubled look on his face said all had not gone well.

"Rebecca didn't just forget her passbook. She doesn't have a stamp in her passbook authorizing her trip here. There was nothing I could do to help her once she admitted that. I did get a promise her case will be brought to trial quickly. She will also be charged with working for you illegally."

"She wasn't working for me," I protested. "She helped out around here because she had nothing to do with her time. She asked for things to do."

"I know that, but the police will find that hard to believe. The charge against you has been changed from obstructing arrest to having a Bantu working illegally on your property. This means that instead of a criminal offense, you are now charged with only a misdemeanor. The difference in sentence is considerable. It's the difference between staying or leaving the country. Of course, you can plead innocent to this charge."

"By the way, what did you say to the police captain that amused him so?" I asked.

"I told him to relax. You weren't dangerous—just a dumb American broad who didn't understand the ways of our country."

"Thanks a lot! You're a great friend!"

"Take your choice. You can be considered dumb and stay, or smart and dangerous and leave."

Rebecca's trial was within the week; the police were true to their word. She was found guilty of illegal entry to the area and working without a permit. If her fine had not been paid, she would have spent six months in jail. She found one week sufficient. I asked her why she had pleaded guilty to the charge of working without a permit.

"I was afraid, Mrs. Peace. They told me I would get out more quickly if I pleaded guilty."

My trial was called within the month. This was the first time I had ever been in a court of law. A friend had come along for moral support. An officer directed me to the front of the courtroom when I asked him for help. The judge was conferring with an aide and took no notice of my presence. I stood before the bench fidgeting uneasily. A friendly looking young.man was sitting at a table to my right. He smiled up at me.

"What am I supposed to do?" I whispered. "I've never been in court before."

"Relax," he said. "It's not too bad. Have a seat. The judge wil be ready in a few minutes."

I sat down and the judge looked up.

"Stand up, young woman, You are in a court of law!"

The friendly young man looked over at me and shrugged.

"This is a great beginning," I thought to myself. I stood up and walked to the witness stand which the judge had pointed out to me.

The Bantu Affairs officer read the charges against me in the same slow, serious manner I had encountered at my back door. I sensed it was a difficult task for him. He was a basically honest man. He knew I had obstructed arrest, yet he was charging me with another crime, one he also considered me guilty of, but which was much less danger-ous to the security of his country. I felt sorry for the man as he heaved a great sigh and sat down. He was merely obeying the commands of men in authority over him.

I just had time to stand to attention in the defendant's dock, when my case was called down. A doctor had ar-rived to testify under oath that, yes, a certain white woman had indeed been raped. He himself had examined her and was sure of it.

I twisted in my chair to look at the young black boy standing behind me in the black section of the courtroom. He stood with hands manacled behind his back, head dropped forward, eyes brimming with tears. He looked on the young side of fifteen.

"Tell this boy," the judge was sying to the interpreter, "that due to the seriousness of the charge against him, he has the right to appeal his case to the supreme court."

The penalty for the rape of a white woman by a black man is usually death in South Africa. I know of no case where a white man has been hanged for raping a black woman.

The room went still as interpreter's and defendant's voices mingled. The interpreter looked up. The boy shrank down.

"He says he doesn't understand what you are talking about, Your Honor."

There were sighs and moans from the visitors' gallery. The small boy was led back to his prison cell. I pulled my mind back to my own situation with difficulty.

"You say the Bantu girl was not working for you, Mrs. Peace. Yet she came to your house on a consistent basis for two months. Did you, at any time, give this girl money?"

"Yes, I gave her five rand on two occasions."

The judge raised his eyebrows. The prosecutor smiled. The prosecutor, to my astonishment, was that same young man who offered me a seat. He was not as friendly now.

"Mrs. Peace, do you really expect this court to believe that you gave this girl ten rand out of the goodness of your heart, rather than for services rendered?"

"No, I do not expect the court to believe I gave Rebecca the money out of the goodness of my heart. *Nor* do I expect this court to believe I would insult a fellow human being by paying them ten rand for two month's work."

The prosecutor had no more to say.

"Case dismissed," said the judge. "Insufficient evidence. And young lady—"

"Yes."

"The next time you appear in this courtroom, wear a hat; not for my sake, but out of respect for the law."

13

"Who is this?" Dick asked. He had just picked up the phone and heard, "Hi."

"It's Jack."

"Jack who? The only Jack I know lives in the United States."

"This is your friend from America speaking."

"Where are you, Jack?"

"In America."

It was hard to believe, as Dick had picked up the phone to Jack's voice. No operator, no "one moment, please," no pause or static, just "Hi."

"What a surprise! To what do I owe the pleasure of this call?"

"Gay and I were just sitting here talking about you guys. We have a vacation in three weeks and can't think of a better place to go visit than South Africa and you. You going to be home?"

"Are you serious?" asked Dick.

"Perfectly."

"You don't plan a trip to Africa in three weeks," Dick said.

"We do. Spontaneous trips are the best. Be seeing you."

By the time we met the Montgomerys at the airport, we had planned their two weeks to show them as much of Natal as possible. We went over the itinerary as we sat on the verandah of a Durban hotel, sipping coffee and looking out at the moon-drenched Indian Ocean. We were all pleased that Dick was able to take time off to go with us.

The two weeks the Peaces and Montgomerys spent together are a kaleidoscope of fascinating memories. There were the days spent with the Samsons on their sugar farm. They are warm, hospitable friends. We spent hours along the Zululand coast finding shells, watching the children romp in the sand, watching the birds do their dances of life. We canoed up the Umfolozie River. When Dick and Jack spotted a herd of hippos, Janet Samson and Dick cautiously paddled back up to observe them. Suddenly a hippo sentry, posted downstream from the herd, charged the canoe swiftly and silently with mouth open. Dick and Janet paddled with amazing speed to the opposite shore, only to be met by a grinning crocodile. Their trip back down the river must have set a record.

"No use telling this story back at the office," sighed Jack. "No one would believe me."

We hiked and rock-climbed in the Berg—Natal's lovely mountains. Bushman paintings were known to be in a cave high up the side of a hill. The way looked long and steep. We decided to attempt it. It *was* a long steep way.

Dick and Lisa, our four-year-old daughter, were the only ones who made it to the top.

"This is one story I won't tell back at the office," said Jack as he sat wiping his face and gasping for breath. "It wouldn't be so humiliating if Lisa hadn't made it!"

One evening, toward the end of their stay, we took the Montgomerys to the home of some Indian friends for a curry dinner. Our friends lived in a two-bedroom apartment. They were an extended family of fourteen. Whenever we visited, even unexpectedly, the rooms were spotlessly clean. How they managed this remains a mystery to me. Mrs. Naido had provided a delicious meal. She made a mild curry in deference to our guests' American palates. Even so, Jack sat red of face, tears streaming from his eyes, as he devoured the food. "Sure," he answered gamely, as he was offered a second plate.

We had warned him it was considered impolite in Indian culture to refuse more food. The hostess would take it as a slight to her cooking. Eating is considered an act of friendship as much as a necessity of life.

Jack and Gay were as surprised as we had been on our first visit when Mrs. Naido and the other female members of the family did not sit down at table with us. "It is not our custom for the women to eat with the men," was the simple explanation. When I had suggested that I should eat in the kitchen with the women, as I too was a woman, they were horrified. "You are a guest in our home. In your culture it is different. You must eat with the men. Some of our people eat the Western way, but we do not feel comfortable with it."

As we were sipping a sweet Indian tea at the end of the meal, Jack turned to Joseph and said, "Tell me what you think of apartheid."

The room became still. Joseph sat thinking, then began speaking in a quiet voice.

"How can I tell you what it means for me? It means being called "boy" at the place I have worked hard for five years by a younger man who has just started work and is already earning more than I am, although he is less qualified. It means having nothing to say when my little girl asks me why a young white man pushes me roughly aside on the street so he can pass. It means living with a fear that gnaws at my strength, a fear that grows from the knowledge of the contempt both black and white hold for us Indians. Jack, I don't know how to talk to you about apartheid. For you apartheid is an ideology. For me it is my moment-by-moment experience of life."

14

The car was parked along the main road in the location. I watched as school children tumbled out of the bus, laughing, chattering, skipping excitedly along the road. They had been released from school and were eager to play. Two hundred yards farther up the road, people were shuffling up to the black hospital. Many walked with hunched shoulders, a visible sign of their inward sighs.

I had been sitting there in the car for twenty minutes. Mrs. Ntonsheni was visiting a relative to break the news of her aunt's death and I had chosen to wait in the car.

Through the window, I could see the valleys and hills of the black location. It was an especially beautiful spot, this location. The natural loveliness of the place made the signs of poverty more stark. Shanty huts don't belong in the garden of Eden. As I watched the children, the old people, the hills alive with sunlight, I was overwhelmed with my love for this marvelous portion of the earth. How rich the land, how diverse and fascinating the people! How good life could be here; how full of fear and despair it is!

My mind whirled with incidents from the past, incidents that illuminate life in South Africa.

There was the morning Mrs. Ntonsheni came in weary, worried.

"It is Mr. Ntonsheni," she said. "He was drunk again last night. Why does he get drunk? He never tells me why he gets drunk."

Mr. Ntonsheni had recently retired. He had worked thirty years for the city, in the garbage detail. For thirty years, five days a week, Mr. Ntonsheni ran after a garbage truck *that never stopped going*, as he emptied the white man's trash. At the end of a day, he was dog-tired. At the end of thirty years he was worn out. Due to his exceptional work record, the city had given him a retirement pension of ten rand per month. It was made clear to him that this was not the usual procedure, but a special recognition for his outstanding service.

"Why does he get drunk, Mrs. Peace? It makes more work for me. We need the money he drinks up to live. Why doesn't he understand it hurts his family?"

"He knows no other way to handle the reality of his

life," I said. "I know it places more burden on you. Perhaps it will help if you understand it is a sign of his own deep pain and frustration."

There was the morning Mrs. Ntonsheni's nephew, Jonathan, came to call. He stopped in periodically to see how she was. I invited him to join me on the verandah for tea. We talked about his plans for the future, his frustrations with the unjust limitations placed on his life. I inquired about his mother's health and we discussed the hard life of a black woman who wants to make a home for her family and fights for it. She lives in constant fear that the home she has worked to maintain can be destroyed by a government edict ordering the women and children to a "homeland" they have never seen. At one point in our conversation Jonathan started to shake his head, then began chuckling.

"What is it?" I asked.

"It's hard to explain," he said. "How could you understand how very strange it is for me to sit here drinking tea with you and talking as we are. It is hard to explain."

There was the afternoon I asked Mrs. Ntonsheni if she had seen my hairbrush. She said she hadn't. Later I found her in the kitchen, quiet with anger.

"What's wrong," I asked.

"I didn't take that hairbrush," she said.

"I never said you did," I replied, surprised and hurt. "I only asked you if you'd seen it. How dare you accuse me of suspecting you of taking it. How could you think such a thing of me?"

"I'm sorry," she said later. "It's an automatic response. If a white woman asks us if we know where something is, she usually thinks we have stolen it and she wants it back. I still feel afraid when you can't find something. Many of my people do steal things. But I think white people expect us to steal or they would pay us enough to live."

There was the evening we had a black friend to dinner. At 7:30 I told Stephen, our three-year-old, it was time to go to bed. He was in the midst of marvelous games with William and was reluctant to leave the fun. Our girls followed him shortly with no more enthusiasm. When I re-entered the living room, having tucked all three children in their beds for the third time, William looked up and spoke.

"This evening I have been related to by white children as a man and a friend, not as a black boy. I do not think it possible for you to comprehend what it has meant to me. Your children have given me a rare gift this evening."

There was the afternoon Mrs. Ntonsheni and I were talking. I answered a knock at the door and returned with a friend. Mrs. Ntonsheni had retreated into the role of silent servant in the few minutes I was away. Once my friend left, I turned to Mrs. Ntonsheni.

"Why don't you let people see who you are? You help perpetuate the silent-servant myth by refusing to show you are a real person."

"You are asking too much of me, Mrs. Peace. I have to protect myself. I can only stand so much pain. If I really showed who I am, most whites in this country would call me 'cheeky.' "

I thought back to one man who had said just that. "That woman is a cheeky servant. I wouldn't have her in my house."

"You have some friends who are different," continued Mrs. Ntonsheni. "When I know I can trust a person, I let them know me. That is as much as I can do."

There was the day I was teaching *Cry, The Beloved Country* by Alan Paton to a class of South African high-school girls.

"I don't like this book, Mrs. Peace."

"Why not, Marie?" I asked.

"Because it makes me feel like Africans are people just like me. If I really believe that, I will have to act different-ly than I do to them. I will have to rethink my plans for my life too."

When we had finished the book, Sally handed me a poem she had written. It was called "This Land of Ours."

They were here first,
But the land was greedily snatched away from them,
And nothing put in its place.
Slowly they drift to the bad world
Of crime, prostitution and drink.

Rich South Africa,
Full of diamonds and gold.
Shares rise,
Men are glad
For them it means more cars, better houses
But the poor African, on whose back the labour's borne,
Still lives in his shabby hut

With his feet for transport
And fire for his warmth.

There were the times we went to visit our friend Geoffry. Legally only two people could be in a room with him at once, for Geoffry was under a banning order. His wife would have to leave the room in order for him not to break his ban. Being caught breaking any of the limitless restrictions on his life resulted in a prison sentence. Geoffry had spent a week in prison for forgetting to report to the police station one Saturday morning for his weekly "check-in." He had slept on a cold concrete floor with one thin blanket. He said he found the week something of a relief. It had released him from being his own jailer.

Geoffry was well educated and was using his forced spare time to work on his doctorate. His jobs varied. They could not break any of the restrictions of his banning order. It was not easy to find a job where he was never in a room with more than two people at a time.

Geoffry was banned at seventeen for voicing his opposition to apartheid in ways that were a "threat to the security of the country." He does not believe in the use of force. The ban was for five years. At the end of five years, he had expected to be rebanned and had prepared himself to face that probability.

He was freed for six months. What I noticed most during that time was that he laughed easily again. At the end of six months he was rebanned. His crime—he had not "changed his ideas" and was still considered "a threat to the government of South Africa."

We asked Geoffry if he had considered leaving the

country on a one-way passport, rather than endure ten years of virtual imprisonment. He *had* considered leaving the country. It was an attractive temptation, for he had much work he wanted to do. Yet he felt at this time his destiny lay in his own land. If his life served for nothing more than to point out what happens to a white South African who loudly opposes apartheid in his country, then so be it.

There was the time a black friend said to me, "Judy, any white man who seriously follows the way of Jesus Christ in our country will eventually end up banned, imprisoned or thrown out of the country. I don't condemn those who don't. It is a *hard* way to live."

There was the time we had dinner with a minister friend in Johannesburg. He told us the story of twenty-two black people he knew, detained in prison for over a year, with no charges brought against them. During this time they were all tortured; men and women. Men's genitals were slammed in drawers and the men left standing there for long periods of time. Women were made to balance on a brick for hours and were beaten when they fell off. Many other horrors were practiced in the hope of getting these people to confess. What they were supposed to confess they never discovered.

When the twenty-two were released, most of them had become committed to violence. Most of them had been pacifists by persuasion upon entering prison. Only a few remained pacifists.

Mrs. Ntonsheni glanced at me as she got back into the car. "You have been crying," she said.

"Yes, I have been feeling the pain of loving this land."

15

The car bumped along over the potholes, slowing when the puddles turned into pools. The first time I had driven this road, I had stopped at the bridge, two wide logs across the swollen stream, and wondered if we could make it across. Today I maneuvered the car across with little hesitation. The road, an oversized cow trail, got progressively worse until we could go no farther. We got out, surrounded by curious, slightly annoyed cows. Few strangers invaded their quiet, lovely pasture, as it was miles from town in an out-of-the-way place.

We looked across the valley shrouded in mist, the lush beauty of the place lost in a vague grayness. The loud calls of people from hill to hill jarred the harmony. Standing here on the heights, no one would suspect this beautiful place housed hundreds of people. People without work. People living in sub-human conditions. People who had lost hope. This was a far cry from the showplace location in Soweto, Johannesburg, the township shown to foreign visitors touring South Africa to see the "true condition" of South Africa's black population.

"It's not too hard to guess why the authorites want whites to stay out of this area," I said to Mrs. Ntonsheni.

"Many people do not know how some of my people must live. If they knew, they would be angry! Come this way. I have found the path down."

We wound down the side of the mountain for half a mile. I never tired of hearing the shouts of the women rise and fall and echo across the valley—a strenuous yet effective communication system.

Mrs. Zuma was not in her hut when we arrived. She was in the church. Her children assured us she would be home soon. We walked to meet her in the direction the daughter, giggling shyly, pointed out. We saw Mrs. Zuma ascending the path supported by a friend. Her sightless eyes shined. I stood in awe of her, for she was joyful in spite of all she was enduring. We greeted one another through Mrs. Ntonsheni. We did not speak one another's language. As we walked, I asked if she had made a decision on the craft school for the blind.

"You must know, I am grateful for this chance, Mrs. Peace. To go to school and learn to weave would be a true pleasure. It would make me feel useful. I could send money back to my children. I would not sit idly in the dark. My son, my daughter and I, we talked. My children said they did not want me to go away, for when they come home now, they find their mother. If I left for the school, they would come home to emptiness. I hope you understand. I know it would be good for me to go, but it is more important for my children to have a mother. They have nothing else."

The next time we visited Mrs. Zuma was to be the last. It was still winter, when life was most hard for her. The children recruited their friends to help unload the coal from the car. Dragging the small sacks down the hillside was laborious. We were women and children and, lacking the strength to carry heavy loads, we made many trips.

Mrs. Zuma's neighbor smiled and nodded her thanks. "This will get her through the rest of the winter. She can cook and keep warm now. She cannot hunt for wood with the rest of us. The children try, but bring little. We all leave her a bit of ours each day, but it is never enough. Now she will be free from worry and cold. God be with you for this."

Mrs. Ntonsheni, Mrs. Zuma and her neighbor chatted in Zulu. I stood looking out over the valley. The air was crisp, cold. I could see my own breath. The sky was a rich blue. The green leaves of the trees framed against the blue made me giddy with their presence. "Look," they seemed to say, "the infinite deep is merely a backdrop for our creation." Slowly I sensed the presence of pain. Mrs. Zuma had never seen her valley. The door to visual adoration was barred to her. Mrs. Zuma was one of the truly great persons I have met. She was a lady of importance to me. My eyes filled with tears as I remembered this was our last visit. Too soon we would leave South Africa. I was overwhelmed with the sense of Mrs. Zuma's helplessness, her aloneness, her utter acceptance of her life.

"Mrs. Ntonsheni," I asked as we entered the hut, "do you think Mrs. Zuma would mind if we prayed together before we go?"

Mrs. Zuma did not mind. There are times to pray. This was one such time. I began a halting, clumsy prayer. The depths of my feelings choked off the words. Words had separated us the year we knew one another. The affection had grown in spite of this. The room was filled with a holy silence, and then my feelings transcended the language barrier. We all felt united, loved, cared for, known. We understood we were at one with one another. It was not easy to pull ourselves away. I chose not to look back as we climbed the winding cow path.

Mrs. Ntonsheni spoke, "Mrs. Zuma said to tell you she did not know she could feel that way with a white woman."

I nodded.

Months after our return to the States, I received a special letter from Mrs. Ntonsheni. "Our friend Mrs. Zuma has died. Her troubles are finished. The neighbors watch the children. The children cannot go to school now. They must work to live. The children say they are alone now; they have lost their mother. They ask, 'Why do we live?' "

16

Too soon our years in South Africa were coming to an end. This had been our place for eight years—our first home together after our marriage, the land of our daughter's birth. We knew it was time to leave, yet we knew we would be leaving much of ourselves behind.

Mrs. Ntonsheni and I avoided the subject, until one day she looked at me. "What can I say to you? You are taking my babies away from me."

"I know," I said. "You are as much a part of their lives as we are. You have given so much of yourself to them and have enriched their lives beyond measure. What can I say to you to ease the pain of their leaving? There is nothing that will make it easy. I don't know how I can leave you myself. We have known one another and worked together for eight years. I don't let myself think of our going."

"Mrs. Peace, we must both think of your going. The time is coming. I will have to work for someone when you leave. My children must eat and go to school. We must think about where I will work. It is better for me to find a new job before you go."

"I have thought of that. I think I can find you a job with one of our friends before we go."

Mrs. Ntonsheni shook her head. "You will not find me a job with your friends."

"Why not? They all know how responsible you are."

"They also see how I am in your house. They will not want me to behave the same in their houses."

"Mrs. Ntonsheni, you are too cynical. Our friends cannot help but see what a good worker you are. They may have changed their perspectives by observing us together."

"I am not cynical, just realistic. You can try to find me a job with one of your friends, but you will fail. Many of them are nice people, but most of them are white South Africans first."

I spent the next few weeks informing friends that Mrs. Ntonsheni needed a job starting the first of July. Some said they would have her if they needed help, which they didn't. A few said they needed help, but wouldn't have her. They preferred having someone they felt comfortable training in the ways of their household. They felt Mrs. Ntonsheni had "too strong a personality" to fit into a different lifestyle. I tried, but I was unable to find Mrs. Ntonsheni a job. I finally accepted defeat and placed an ad in the local paper. "Responsible black woman wants housework. Excellent references available." With excellent references, it is not hard to find work. Mrs. Ntonsheni soon had the security of a monthly paycheck once we were gone.

The day we were to leave arrived. How does one leave a place that has been home and people who have been friends. The time had come for Mrs. Ntonsheni and me to say goodbye.

I looked at Mrs. Ntonsheni.

"Life is made up of meeting and parting, of saying hello and goodbye," she said, and looked away.

"How can I leave you?" I thought to myself. We had been together for eight years. We had felt anger and affection, cautiousness and trust, distance and warmth, frustration and enjoyment, depression and hope. We had felt alien to one another and we had felt known by one another. Our lives had become interdependent in so many ways, even while we had feared this. In eight years, we had come to love one another. I embraced Mrs. Ntonsheni. "I cannot say goodbye to you. It is too hard for me."

"It is too hard for me," she said. "I have dreaded the coming of this day."

We both wept.

She left me standing alone in the garden. Walking slowly, with head erect, she passed through the gate. She did not look back.

Months passed. We were settled into our new home. The children were making friends. Dick and I were beginning to feel a part of our new community. Mrs. Ntonsheni and I were corresponding. I knew she had had three jobs since our leaving. One day a letter arrived informing me she had found a new position.

"This woman is from England, Mrs. Peace. She seems very nice. I think I will like working for her. I hope so."

I hoped so too. She had felt restless and dissatisfied since our departure. It had made me feel guilty. Perhaps Mrs. van der Merwe was right. My mind wandered back to the day we attended a *braaivleis* at her home. It was a spring day in Johannesburg. The sun was brilliant, the sky cloudless. The garden was lush with varieties of plants and flowers. The van der Merwes were warm people, people committed to breaking down the barriers between the English and the Afrikaners. They were one of the first Afrikaans families I met living in a predominantly English community. Apartheid is a cultural, as well as racial, attitude toward life. I respected the van der Merwes for choosing to reach beyond their cultural heritage. This was not done lightly by an Afrikaner. Their cultural roots were deep, emotional and brought inner stability to the business of living.

Mrs. van der Merwe and I were in the midst of devouring sausages straight off the grill. We were discussing the problem of hiring good help.

"I'm lucky to have a woman working with me who has become a real friend," I said.

Mrs. van der Merwe turned her head to look at me. "How much are you paying your servant?"

I was surprised by the question, but I answered.

"That is far too much," she said. "You are making it impossible for her to be satisfied with a normal work situation. You are spoiling her for her place in our society. Every person must accept their lot in life realistically and be content with life as it is. Mrs. Ntonsheni is being ruined for life as a black woman in South Africa. You are doing her no favor."

"Is it wrong to try to act justly in the midst of injustice?" I asked.

"You don't understand. It is a matter of facing reality, not a matter of justice."

"I cannot feel it is hurting her to see her family fed and to send her children to school," I said. "What she has now cannot be taken away from her even if life is harder in the years ahead."

Yet today I feel guilt, for Mrs. Ntonsheni is now dissatisfied. She was not content with the injustice of her life before we met. Have we made it more unbearable for her? I do not know. I only know I would act the same again.

17

It looked innocent enough. Just a thin, blue air-mail letter pushed through the mail slot in our front door. Since living in Africa, we had received many such letters. I switched off the vacuum cleaner, bent to pick up the fragile paper and settled down in a chair to catch up on the life and thoughts of a friend. From the handwriting, I saw this was a letter from Mrs. Ntonsheni. I carefully pried open the glued paper and read with anticipation.

Anticipation gave way to shock. When I finished the letter, I sat quietly, stunned. Slowly the quiet was invaded by the emotion that welled up from deep within me and burst forth into sobs.

This is what I had read:

Dear Mr. & Mrs. Peace & family,

I hope you have heard the sad news about my loving daughter, Rebecca. She passed away on the 25th of September. She was knocked down by a car on the location's main road. She died on arrival at the hospital. We did love Rebecca very much. She was really a sweet child of the family. But God loved her also to come by His side. I do wish you would really pray for us. I think if you were still here Rebecca shouldn't have had this accident because she would have come with me to work.

I'm not going to work for these people, Mrs. Lewis, anymore because she was cross with me because I stayed at home till the funeral. She wanted me to come to work. I am very sick and very weak since Rebecca's death. I want to stay home till I feel well and get sure that I will never see Rebecca again.

I wish you were all here in these days of sadness. I won't forget this easily because I can't believe Rebecca is dead.

Give my love to all the family.

Love,
Mrs. Ntonsheni & family

Finally my grief was drained of emotion and my mind took over, whirling with thoughts. Rebecca, only seven at the time of her death, was the youngest of Mrs. Ntonsheni's eight children. She was especially loved by the other members of the family, for she was "the baby" to all of them. Why did it have to be Rebecca? I thought of the fun she and Lisa and Jenny had had playing. Rebecca had been very shy when Mrs. Ntonsheni had first brought her to our home. But soon she was running and shouting and playing with our girls. Prejudice must be taught and these three children quickly and naturally became good friends. Rebecca's death would be hard for Lisa and Jenny to understand.

I thought of Mrs. Lewis. Mrs. Ntonsheni had been full of hope when she started working for her: "She is a nice woman, Mrs. Peace. She is from England. I hope this job works out."

I had hoped it would work out too. Yet I remembered something Mrs. Ntonsheni had told me long before.

"My people think it is sometimes easier to work for white South Africans than for people from England and America. People from overseas say they think apartheid is wrong. They act very nice to us at first. Soon they get used to the ways of our country. It does not seem too bad to them anymore. They like having servants cheaply. Before long they expect more of us than our whites do. When we work for white South Africans, we know what is expected of us. They grow up being taught the way they should treat their servants. We don't like the way we are treated, but we know what to expect and how to survive with them. Americans and Englishmen can talk nice, but they can get very hard toward us, living in our land."

I couldn't help feeling that many white South Africans would have accepted and understood Mrs. Ntonsheni's need to grieve her daughter's death at home among her family. Mrs. Lewis, a nice Englishwoman, had come to see Mrs. Ntonsheni as the object that freed herself from manual labor. She had become angry when her easy lifestyle was interrupted by Mrs. Ntonsheni's own human needs.

A few weeks later I received another letter from Mrs. Ntonsheni. She explained that Rebecca had been killed by a hit-and-run driver. The family had gone to the police station to find out who had killed their daughter. When a policeman was asked if he could find the information for them, he had looked at them impatiently. "Don't you know we have more important things to do with our time than to keep records of everyone who is killed? We know nothing of your daughter's death!"

"Mrs. Peace," wrote Mrs. Ntonsheni, "the way that policeman treated us, we could have been speaking about the death of a dog. Why is our country this way?"

18

There was a day, in the city of Johannesburg, when Samuel and I sat down to talk. We had talked before. It had become a part of our daily ritual, sitting at the kitchen table for a cup of tea and talk.

Samuel kept the garden for the house we were renting. He was there when we arrived. We had come to know one another over the past year. You can learn a surprising amount over a morning cup of tea. One of the things I had learned was that Samuel was a frustrated composer.

"Mrs. Peace," he asked one day, "do you know how to write down notes for music?"

"Not very well," I answered. "Why do you ask?"

"I have music going on in my head all the time. It begs to be let out. I do not know how to let it out. Sometimes while I am riding my bicycle it gets so strong I think I will burst. When I am working in the garden, I feel quiet. That is why I love the garden. The rest of the time the music bothers me, wanting me to let it live for others, impatient with me for keeping it locked up inside my head. I have tried to find a place to learn to let the music out. I can find no such place for a black man like me. Do you know of a place?"

I knew of no such place. I also knew if one could find such a place, it would be expensive, far beyond Samuel's means.

"Samuel, it is terrible to consider the artistic talent among your people that has been lost to the world because of the false limitations placed on your lives."

"Yes," Samuel replied, "it is a truly terrible thing."

This particular morning we were sipping our tea and discussing Joe. Joe had entered South Africa illegally in order to find work. He was from Malawi. He had come to us for help. While we could not offer him work, we did give him a place to sleep at night. Joe had not found work. He spent his time drinking and fighting. We finally persuaded him that he was foolish to stay in South Africa.

"Joe," I had said, "you cannot find work in South Africa without a permit. You cannot get a permit without legal entry into the country."

"If I had entered the country legally, I would have to work in the mines," said Joe. "That I could not do."

"Why do you stay here?" I asked. "You will never find work."

"There is no work for me at home. I cannot sit and watch my family starve."

"You are not sending your family money. Now they have no food and no father. You drink and fight in Johannesburg. One day you may die on the street. Will that help your family?"

Joe had been convinced he would be of more use to himself and his family at home and we had put him on the train with a great sense of relief.

"It is a good thing that Joe went home," Samuel was saying. "It is dangerous to live in Johannesburg. Many men die here. Boys come from the country to make their fortune in the city. There are not enough jobs for all who come to Johannesburg. If you are black, you must have a permit to live in Johannesburg. Yet my people come without permits, for permits are hard to get unless you go to the mines. It is very hard to work in the mines. It is a living death to my people.

"Some men will not go to the mines. They will not sit in the homeland without work and watch their families starve either. They come to Johannesburg illegally. They find no work. They turn to drinking, stealing, killing. Black men from other countries are not liked, for our own men cannot find work. Joe will live longer at home. It is a good thing that he went back. It is a terrible place, this city of Johannesburg. It is a beautiful place, this city of gold. Johannesburg is a place of wealth and promise, a place of poverty and despair. It is a terrible place, this country of South Africa. It is a beautiful place, this country of mine."

Samuel and I sat and were silent, both lost in our own thoughts. Suddenly Samuel looked up. His gaze was intense.

"Mrs. Peace, you must wonder how my people endure all the suffering, all the oppression heaped upon them in this their country, their home."

"Yes, I have often wondered at it."

"We are a people of patience and hope. While we have hope, we can endure with patience almost anything. We still have hope. Our hope is this: that God cannot ignore our cries of suffering that come before him daily. He will free us from our imprisonment in our own land. We see America as the country that believes in men's freedom. We hope that America will be used to free us. America will not allow us to suffer so, but will fight for our freedom."

"Samuel, it is a hard thing I have to tell you. You must not place too much hope in America. America has much money invested in your country. It is in her interest to see your government remain stable and in control. I do not believe America will fight for your freedom. I may be wrong, but you must not place your hope there.

"Surely God hears your cries. He is a God of justice, of truth, of righteousness and of patience. The oppressor cannot win in the end, yet the end can still be far off. History moves toward truth and justice, yet history moves exceedingly slowly."

Samuel sat with slumped shoulders and downcast eyes. When he looked up, I could see he was old and tired.

"Mrs. Peace, I said that as long as my people have hope they can endure anything. Yet the day they lose all hope, they would rather fight and die than go on living. My people are beginning to lose hope, Mrs. Peace. Their patience is being drained away. Their endurance is faltering. The end of this chapter of our story may not be far off. I pray with all good men that reason, not violence, will be the vehicle for our justice. May God have mercy on us all."

There was a day, in the city of Johannesburg, six years ago, when Samuel and I sat down to talk. It is my hope that the patience endures and the talking continues; that reason will win over fear, and violence will be cheated by the positive action of love.

19

God sets before us life and death and says, "Choose life."

In June of 1976, the children of Soweto, the African township outside Johannesburg, stopped and looked at their lives. They said in their hearts, No more, we have had enough. One day, the children of Soweto walked out into the streets in protest at the wrongs heaped upon them in the place of their birth. The children walked out into the streets and died.

They were protesting the mandatory use of Afrikaans in the schools. They wanted English. English is a universal language, they said. Afrikaans is not relevant in today's world. It is a language of isolation, they said.

The children knew it was illegal to demonstrate. They

knew policemen with dogs and clubs, gas and guns would be present. Yet they marched in protest.

Some were killed. People said how awful that the children were killed. What is this country coming to ? Afrikaans was dropped as a mandatory language in South African schools.

It has been said that a little child shall lead them. The children of Soweto crossed an invisible, yet profound line that day in June. They looked at their options and chose death. Is the shedding of blood necessary, after all, for the freedom of a people?

In 1977 Steve Biko, a young, intelligent spokesman for black South Africa, died in prison in South Africa. On October 27, an inquest into his death was held. During that inquest it was revealed that the night before his death, Mr. Biko had been moved, naked and in chains, from Port Elizabeth to Pretoria, a distance of 750 miles. The autopsy showed Biko died of severe brain damage, impaired blood circulation and acute kidney failure. He also had two broken ribs. Yet the white South African judge cleared the state of any guilt in the death of Mr. Biko.

After the verdict of not guilty had been handed down, an old African man stood outside the courthouse. The old man stood with his head down, turning his hat around in his hands, around and around in his hands. "This is a terrible thing the white man has done today. A terrible, terrible thing. We do not want violence, we want peace. So why does the white man do this to us? Doesn't he *know* that we want peace?"

What a people want may not be what a people choose. Years ago a black South African said to me, "I live with fear in the land of my birth. I am treated as a child in my own country. To let go of the fear, to become free within myself, could cost me my life. But my executioner would know he was killing a man."

PART TWO

20

The bishop waited patiently for the child to reply. It is no small thing for a twelve-year-old girl to answer such questions. He returned her open, direct gaze. Innocence and pain are hard to meet in a child's eyes, even for a bishop.

No, she finally said, she had not wanted to move to this place. What kind of a person would choose to move to this desolate spot in the Ciskei far from home? she wondered but was too polite to ask. She and her mother had not been asked if they wanted to come here. Government troops simply arrived in the village one morning and herded the people onto trucks, dumping them off in the midst of this arid land.

"Does your mother have work?" the bishop asked.

"No," said the child. Her mother had no work. But that was not surprising, as few of the women living here were able to find work.

"Since there is no work to be found, does the government provide you with a pension on which to survive?" the bishop asked.

"No, the government does not provide us with a pension," said the child.

"With no work and no pension from the government, how do you and your mother eat?" asked the bishop.

"We borrow food," replied the child with heartbreaking simplicity.

"And when you are unable to borrow food?" the bishop gently probed.

"Then I drink a lot of water and pray to God that my stomach doesn't hurt too much."

Bishop Desmond Tutu, former president of the South African Council of Churches, the present bishop of Johannesburg and winner of the Nobel Peace Prize, has been a witness to brutality and injustice in many forms in his land. This small girl's simple acceptance of her fragile survival in this latest of the world's ghettos struck his heart at its very center. This child, bound to her empty, swollen belly, was the bearer of apartheid. A heavy load for such a small frame.

The Homeland Policy is foundational to the apartheid structure. "People are destined to live their lives within their own tribes, maintaining the purity of their ethnic heritage, their unique traditions and values," says the South African government. The solution? "Separate but equal development."

South Africa's black population accounts for 72 percent of South Africa's people. They have been given 13 percent of the land for the black "Homelands," much of it economically unviable. The average salary for a person residing in a Homeland is under $100 per year. The unemployment rate is over 30 percent and as high as 80 percent, depending on how you calculate it. It is clear that the young girl Bishop Tutu spoke with is only one of a large number of children who make up the statistics on malnutrition and starvation in these "independent states."

Over three million black South Africans have been uprooted in the past twenty years. This dispossession is justified as the only way to bring a lasting peace to a complex society. Is it unreasonable to ask people to sacrifice for the sake of their country's survival? white politicians ask. The sacrifice they call for is made by other people.

Most South African whites never witness or participate in the sacrifices they demand from others. They never see the four-year-old child sitting on an ash heap near the barbed wire fence that encloses her "Homeland." The fence is outlined against the sky at night by harsh white lights. The child sits stuffing ashes into her mouth with quick, desperate movements. Perhaps she hopes the ashes will bring relief from the terrible hunger that gnaws at her body. The child's hunger will go unnoticed by the larger world. Many kinds of fences will keep it hidden.

Most of South Africa's white citizens live their lives a safe distance, geographically and psychologically, from the suffering resulting from the Homeland Policy. They see it as a necessary policy that helps preserve peace.

It is easy to understand why the world focuses on South Africa. The cruelty of apartheid is self-evident. Dr. Allan Boesak, a leading opponent of apartheid in the South African "colored" community, has experienced its barbs in particularly painful ways. One could understand if he concentrated all his energy on this one manifestation of evil in our world. But Dr. Boesak feels a responsibility to fight against all fear that brings "the destruction of God's world." He does not limit his call to the fight against apartheid in his own country. He speaks out against the "madness of militarism" he sees surfacing around the world.

America has embarked on the largest military buildup ever undertaken in a time of "peace." Is America's armed stance against the world very different from the white

South African government's position toward black South Africans? Black South Africans are being forced, due to the military might of their government, to exist on a small portion of their native land, while a white minority enjoys the bulk of their country's wealth.

South Africa suffers from apartheid, America from patriotic nationalism. Both adhere to policies of domination. Domination is based on fear. Remove the fear of force from a people and you must replace domination with an equality based on mutual respect and understanding. But understanding takes time. To understand, one must listen. Listening to others as equals is hard and painful, as well as slow. It appears to be easier, more efficient, to those who hold military might, to rule as masters. But the cost of such a path is very high, as South Africa is learning.

The dividends of listening are many. In the give and take of communication, people and nations can share rich treasures of knowledge out of the storehouses of their unique histories. New insights emerge; old weaknesses are exposed.

21

He was bursting with the eager energy of a sixteen year old. The measured, care-filled words caught me off guard.

"My parents were tribal people. They were raised according to the old ways. For them, the community was the extended family. They had many fathers and mothers, sisters and brothers."

The young man's words remind me of a story told to me by the late Colin Winter, who was then bishop of Namibia.

An African friend asked me to baptize his mother. No small request, as it required a ten-mile hike across desert to reach her. She lived in a remote area inaccessible by car. I was happy to do this for my friend, and the walk gave us time to be together and talk.

The woman I baptized upon our arrival was not my friend's mother. I said nothing, simply performing the ceremony. As we trekked back home, I asked my friend why he had told me it was his mother who wanted to be baptized. "Were you afraid I wouldn't have walked that far for someone else?" I asked. "I would have come with you anyway."

My friend looked puzzled. "That was my mother, Colin."

"I've met your mother and that woman was a stranger," I replied.

"Colin, one day I found that old woman wandering alone in the bush, lost and confused. I knew God had sent me another mother to take care of."

The young man interrupted my remembering as he continued with his story.

"The people of my tribe assumed it was hard and required much wisdom to raise a child. To leave such a task to one man and one woman simply because they bore the child would be to lack common sense. They understood the birth process does not automatically equip a father and a mother with the diversity of tools needed to nurture a dependent baby into a mature adult. Such a process requires an infinite amount of affection. Such a process requires years of patient training in one's duty to the community, one's duty to one's neighbors and one's duty to oneself. It takes an entire village to give a child all it requires to become a contributing human being.

"Village elders, chosen for their wisdom, are appointed the children's teachers. Others shower the young with attention. This is a task undertaken with genuine joy. Is this not the reason we live, to give our love to the next generation?

"My father was trained well in many things. He lived among bare-breasted women, having the internal discipline of mind necessary to treat them with appropriate respect and care. 'You young men,' he said, 'you see a woman's underwear hanging out to dry and you have trouble with lustful thoughts.' My father was trained well in many things, but no one taught my mother and him how to parent a child alone. When the white culture came up against the tribal system, the tribal system was destroyed. You cannot rebuild what is already gone.

"When I was a child, the tribe was already finished. My parents could not tap the wisdom that had been available to their parents. To raise a child on their own was beyond their understanding. The white culture destroyed our customs but put nothing new in place of the old. This school has become my parent. Here I learn how I must live."

The young man stopped talking, surprised he had revealed so much to a white woman he had just met. His openness and self-knowledge were unusual for a teenager. But he was living in unusual times.

"What has the school taught you?" I asked him.

"Here I have learned to accept the truth about myself," he replied.

"And what is that truth?" I dared to ask.

"I am a man without a culture, a man without a home," he said. "My roots have been torn away from me. The plant that nourished my parent's lives has already shriveled for lack of soil. But many fruits from the plant still live. It is my task to embrace the good fruits from my heritage, while accepting that I cannot retreat into a past that no longer exists."

"Will you join the white culture?" I asked.

"For me the white culture is the wrong path. Your culture has come to understand many of the wonders of science. But your culture has not yet learned to live well as human beings. In pursuing your goals for the future, you have lost the joy of the moment. In trying to understand the origins of life, you have lost the capacity to celebrate the gift of life. No, I will not become a part of the white culture."

"What, then, will you do?"

The young man signed with a heaviness beyond his years.

"I cannot find it in my heart to embrace the systems of the East or the West. Both have already been judged and found wanting by history. I cannot stay where I am, in a place that is no place. I have no choice but to forge a new way. This is a hard truth of mine. But with God's help, all things are possible."

"I wish you well," I said quietly.

He gave me a slight smile. "Limbo is a frightening place to be. Limbo is also an exhilarating place to be. One understands a person cannot stay there. One knows the only possible movement is a step forward."

A step forward sounds simple. In reality, it is exceedingly hard. When the old has been swept away, treasures can be lost and voids can surface.

Mrs. Ntonsheni once told me that my country had two institutions that her people, the Zulus, would never allow in their midst. She believed that a civilized nation had no need of orphanages and old age homes. "Our people would not allow any human being to be homeless," she said. She believed that a culture that did not care for its weak and lonely was a culture that had lost its heart. She assumed an institutionalized person was an uncared-for person.

How could a person be getting the love and care he or she deserved from an institution? How could a person, with all of his or her unique history, be known in such a place? Without a home, one is homeless. This she knew. A good people provide homes. This she also knew.

Years ago, when an elderly aunt had grown old and unable to care for herself, Mrs. Ntonsheni had taken her into her own home and cared for her aunt as she would have cared for her own mother. What Mrs. Ntonsheni knew was true was what Mrs. Ntonsheni lived.

I recently received a letter from Mrs. Ntonsheni, who is now in the winter of her own life. "My eldest sister, who was living in Durban, passed away on the 31st of May, this year. I thank God for her because she was old and sick and had no one to look after her. God has given her a rest."

For Mrs. Ntonsheni's sister, an "uncivilized" old age home would have been an improvement over her discardment. I sensed Mrs. Ntonsheni's pain, the pain of having lived long enough to see life among her people come to such a place as this.

22

Mrs. Ntonsheni once told me that she wished Shaka still lived. "If Shaka were alive, the white people would not dare to treat us the way they do. If Shaka were alive, our people would live as they should."

"If Shaka were alive, your life would probably be in danger," I replied. "Shaka tolerated no independent thinking or action from his subjects."

Shaka, early chief of the Zulu tribe, forged the largest, strongest nation on the southern tip of Africa, using an inflexible discipline backed by force. Soldiers who did not dance with enough spirit had their necks broken instantly. Shaka's training methods produced soldiers of prodigious strength and discipline. He believed his tough regime was necessary to build the Zulus into the great nation they were "destined to become."

The young men lived together in dormitories. If they proved themselves worthy warriors, they were allowed to marry at the age of thirty. Girls were formed into regiments that cooked and nursed for the warriors and mended their weapons. Shaka turned the Zulu nation into a formidable war machine that no other tribe dared attack.

The life of a member of Shaka's tribe was safe and predictable—as long as one kept in one's place. Life was neither safe nor predictable for members of the lesser tribes in the region. The threat of annihilation or domination was a constant terror.

Tribalism appears secure only to those whose tribe is dominant. Their security is more fragile than it seems. When a tribe has great power, the leaders are tempted to use the laws of the land to control their own people. It is easy for such leaders to forget that their task is to seek justice for the people. The more unlimited the leaders' power, the stronger the temptation to use violence for the sake of control. The antidote for such an abuse of power is the people's acceptance of their responsibility. It is the people who hold their government accountable for an open and just rule.

Shaka did not provide an open society for the Zulus. That was not their expectation. There is disagreement as to whether the society was "just." Shaka did provide a secure fortress for the Zulus. Yet it was from within that fortress that the challenge to Shaka's power arose.

Shaka's people had been tolerant of his great control, for he had provided them with a strong national identity, along with a reliable way of life. The people's tolerance wavered when Shaka started infringing on the territory of the diviner, the priest in the tribe. In taking upon himself the role of the diviner, Shaka caused a serious upset in the balance of power. Shaka had taken absolute control. His tyranny grew. Shaka was known to have men impaled for merely coughing in his presence.

A time came when the people could no longer tolerate Shaka's slide into cruelty and irrationality in his use of violence for control. Shaka was assassinated. Dingane, his half brother, became chief. Shaka's reign was brought to an end from within his own tribe.

On July 21, 1985, South Africa declared a state of emergency. This was necessary, said the government, to maintain law and order.

In response to this act, a small group of white South Africans took upon themselves the responsibility of visiting black townships to gather statements from the people. They saw it as their task to expose the "law and order" that was being maintained.

"We were sitting in our home," said one woman. "Suddenly the door flew open and several policemen burst in, shouting, 'Botha told us we can kill you like flies.' The policemen attacked us, very brutally. We all ended up with cuts across our faces and chests. These were bad cuts, up to one inch deep. Even our sister, who was six months pregnant, was not spared this nightmare."

When asked why they had been singled out for this assault, the family had no answer. By anyone's definition, they were peaceful, law-abiding citizens.

A white South African, on holiday in the States, is on the other end of the telephone line.

"These must be hard, painful times for you in your country," said my husband.

"Life is still good in South Africa," the man replied. "Your newspapers overstate the situation. The unrest is limited to the black townships [places outside white cities where black South Africans who have work in white urban areas live]. The government has control. No need to be overly worried—the agitators will soon be silenced."

23

On Wednesday, September 4th, 1985, three hundred school children of "mixed race" marched to a shopping center in downtown Cape Town. The children carried anti-apartheid signs and sang "We Are the World." The police, without apparent warning, started clubbing the teenagers with riot batons. The police chased the youth up a main street in Cape Town, whipping them with four-foot-long plastic whips.

"Some of these kids were so badly whipped that their shirts were shredded and covered with blood. One girl fell and two big, hulking policemen just stood over her and whipped her for a full minute. These weren't big kids, but probably thirteen, fourteen and fifteen years old. It is hard to see how singing 'We Are the World' warranted this action," said a passing businessman.

Cape Town's white office workers and shopkeepers watched the brutal attack with horror. The teenagers, they knew, were members of Cape Town's generally conservative "colored" community. These kids had not been known for radical behavior in the past. Singing "We Are the World" in a white section of Cape Town was an act of great courage for these adolescents. It was probably the most daring, and possibly the first, protest they had ever made.

It was an act of frustrated rage when hundreds of black South Africans went on a four-hour rampage in downtown Johannesburg.

A group of blacks formed a half circle around a young white woman holding a baby in her arms. The woman, screaming, backed up against the window of a store. The people in the mob smashed the window with bottles, bricks and clubs. Yet they did not touch the terrified woman or her child.

A middle-aged white woman, holding the hand of a young boy no more than twelve years old, was chased until she fell. She and the boy were kicked and punched by the group of people who surrounded them. The woman and boy crawled into a grocery store, where they were not pursued. They had been badly shaken and physically hurt, but their lives had been spared.

White merchants who tried to stop looting were beaten, badly. Stones were thrown at the police. A policeman was stabbed in his right shoulder. But no white person was killed.

The original group of black protestors was quickly joined by thousands of black passersby, who began filling the streets. Police with dogs tried to scatter the crowds. The police, who were strongly outnumbered, were unable to control the crowds. It was the arrival of the army that convinced the people to disperse.

This confrontation, on October 18, 1985, carried a great weight. It was the first time that black South Africans had fought the South African police force on white territory. What had brought the people to the place where they were willing to cross this line?

That day, Benjamin Moloise, a thirty-year-old black upholsterer and poet, had been hanged at dawn. The gov-

ernment had convicted Moloise of killing a black policeman. Mr. Moloise admitted helping plan the murder for
the African National Congress (A.N.C.). He insisted to the
end that he was not the killer.

A black policeman believed to be collaborating with
the enemy was an especially vulnerable target for the
A.N.C. The policeman lived among the very people who
considered him a traitor. His skin color, not his politics,
determined his place of residence. The Group Areas Act of
1950 made that quite clear.

The white South African government would use a
black man's skills. The white South African government
would not protect a black man's life. Not if it meant going
against their own ideology.

The African National Congress had recently decided
they would strike at "civilian targets as well as at military
and economic institutions." This simply meant they had
decided to kill people as well as blow up buildings. The
A.N.C. had grown tired of watching their members killed
by the South African police. "No longer will they do all
the killing, while we do all the suffering," they said.

Outside the prison walls, where her son would die,
Benjamin Moloise's mother held a death watch. She had
been refused permission to see Benjamin on the morning
of his dying.

"I begged. I said, it's the last time. That's my son. This
government is cruel. It is really cruel."

Perhaps the government hoped the hanging would
scare the people into submission.

Benjamin Moloise once wrote: "A storm of oppression
will be followed by the rain of my blood. I am proud to
give my life, my solitary life."

Benjamin Moloise gave his life for helping to plan the

taking of life. One hopes he accomplished more than his executioners did.

24

There is a special revulsion, a physical way we recoil upon hearing that a person has harmed one of his or her "own kind." We experience the same instinctive disgust we felt the first time we learned about cannibalism.

"This woman is an informer," the man shouted, as he pointed his finger at the instantly terrified human being. The woman froze, her body assuming the posture of a trapped animal. Her response was instinctive. She had little time to comprehend what was about to happen to her. Her eyes, wide with fright, darted first here, then there, frantically searching for a way out. Any glimmer of hope quickly faded. People were circling her, closing in, creating a density and a depth with their human wall that made even an attempt to escape futile.

Suddenly a man broke forward and doused the woman with gasoline from the can he was holding. For an instant the crowd, acting as one, seemed to hold its breath. Did they, just for that moment, feel the awful weight of the deed in which they were about to participate?

The moment passed; the possibility of grace was gone. A heavy rubber tire, doused with gasoline, was flung around the woman's neck. Someone lighted a match and

77

without the slightest hesitation flung this instrument of death onto the flesh of the woman who was pinned to the ground.

The flash of fire was instantaneous. The woman's death agonies were not.

Bishop Desmond Tutu, addressing a crowd at a mass funeral in a black township where fifteen local people had died in recent "police actions," denounced the government for its brutality. The bishop then raised his voice and, with deep emotion, condemned the woman's burning.

"Our cause is just and noble. That is why it will prevail and bring victory to us. We cannot use methods to attain the goal of liberation that our enemy will use against us. Many people around the world support us. When they saw that woman burning on television, they must have said that maybe we are not ready for freedom."

At the end of my talk on South Africa, a gentleman near the front asked, "Are South African blacks capable of ruling their land yet? Aren't the people still too tribal, too primitive to have political control? It takes a special brutality to burn a woman alive."

Tribalism energizes some power in South Africa. Zulus still fight members of the Pondo tribe. For over fifty years the African National Congress has worked hard to replace tribal consciousness with a strong national identity among black South Africans. A.N.C. leaders understood that a divided people could not stand against the strong fortress being built by the Afrikaners.

The white South African government has labored hard

to strengthen tribalism, structurally as well as psychologically. The Homelands are crucial to their success. The Afrikaners have long understood that a tribal consciousness works to strengthen the whites and weaken the blacks. The five million whites sprang from two tribes. The twenty-four million blacks were birthed from ten.

The government has a certain advantage in this warfare. The instinctual survival needs of a group can overwhelm the more human need to reach out.

The event did not make the headlines; it was mentioned almost as an aside: Fifteen white Afrikaans students at the University of Potchefstroom had assaulted and tortured an English-speaking student. The tortured young man was a member of a student group the Afrikaans students considered dangerously liberal. As these human beings consciously, methodically inflicted pain upon another person's flesh, a person helpless in their power, they explained to him that he was getting what he deserved, as he was a "bad white who belonged in Soweto" (the black township outside Johannesburg).

Tribalism can fuel hatred and acts of violence even without the help of mob hysteria. If asked, the boys would no doubt deny that this "incident" was a matter of Afrikaners versus English. For them it was a question of loyalty—white supporting white against the "black peril."

Much like the woman's burning. That, too, was a question of loyalty.

I live in a country whose best minds have imagined weapons of unthinkable destruction. I live in a country whose hands have built missiles capable of annihilating all the peoples of the earth. I live in a country whose government considers it a "question of loyalty" if one protests this dark squandering of the gifts of mind and will and spirit. My country believes that such brutal tools for the inflicting of pain are necessary. We must defend ourselves against the terrors of the "red menace."

I live in a country capable of comtemplating the killing of the children of Moscow for the sake of the survival of our own American tribe. I need not ask myself how Afrikaans students could torture an Englishman. I know whence their impulses sprang.

25

A friend of Steve Biko, the martyred South African activist, told this story.

Biko was driving through the Transkei. He noticed two Afrikaans teenagers walking along a lonely stretch of road. He stopped and offered them a lift, happy for the company. The boys sat huddled awkwardly in the back seat. They spoke only in response to Steve's questions, their answers formulated in a hesitant, broken English.

Steve finally switched to Afrikaans and asked the boys why they were speaking to him in English when it was so hard for them. "Obviously," he said, "your language is Afrikaans."

The boys glanced at each other with a look of relief. "We thought you, being a black man, would be angry with us if we spoke Afrikaans," said one of the boys.

"Why would a man be angry at a person for using his own language?" asked Steve Biko. "You must never be ashamed of your language. Use it with great pride."

Love, not shame, reveals the truth. A people who love themselves enough to face themselves are a people capable of celebrating their heritage by transcending it.

26

Eight Afrikaans students recently decided to accept a standing invitation for informal talks from the youth wing of the African National Congress in Lusaka, Zambia, the headquarters-in-exile of the A.N.C. President Botha of South Africa ordered the students' passports revoked, preventing them from leaving the country.

The Afrikaans students all attend Stellenbosch, South Africa's equivalent of Harvard or Yale. "We are moderate, concerned Afrikaners," said the group's leader, a twenty-two-year-old law student. "We are trying to be realistic. Ninety percent of the people in Soweto support the A.N.C. It doesn't help to deny they exist. It's an infamous lie that all blacks in this country hate whites and vice versa. You can only get through this myth if you get together and talk."

A second student responding to President Botha's effective banning of their planned talks said, "Dialogue is the only way we can get out of this mess, and to have that stopped is sad. The A.N.C. is as much concerned about peace as we are."

Nelson Mandela was born the son of a South African chief. As the eldest boy, it was his destiny to replace his father as head of the Tembu tribe.

History intervened. Mandela lived to see the place of his birth transformed into an "independent Homeland" run by the white South African government. The chief's role was reduced to being little more than the mouthpiece for the tribe's new masters.

Mandela understood he had been born into a world that was doomed. It was a world he chose to leave, so that his people could be renewed. Educated as a lawyer, Mandela was a driving force behind the founding of the Youth League of the African National Congress. He believed that black South Africans, united by their common birthright, could help forge their country's future.

Mandela helped organize the Defiance Campaign of 1952. This was a time when 8,500 volunteers deliberately went to jail for breaking the hated pass laws. This action was consciously taken to confront the state with its unjust ways; it was an action of nonviolent protest.

The state's response to such activities was to ban mass meetings, demonstrations and political organizing. When the African National Congress's methods were declared illegal, Mandela went underground in order to continue his work—a simple, profoundly hard step to take.

Nelson Mandela has paid a high price for working toward a more just and united structure for the land of his birth. He has served over twenty years of a life prison sentence. The charges against him: treason against the state.

This man, born to be a chief, has become a symbol of hope for many South Africans, both black and white. He is a leader capable of helping his country take its first faltering steps toward its future.

Percy Qoboza, a contemporary of Mandela's and former editor of *The World*, South Africa's leading black newspaper until it was stopped publishing, said, "If the South African government does not negotiate with us, there will be no one left to negotiate with. We are the last generation of black South Africans willing to negotiate."

27

A deputy editor of the black newspaper *Sowetan* said that the black middle class has become a convenient target for the raging black youth who run out of ready victims. "If they are living in shacks and they look across the road and see someone who has a swimming pool, they naturally explode. I would do the same thing. It makes sense if you think it fully through."

A black consultant for Kodak speaks. "The majority of people still live cheek-by-jowl with the impoverished. The seeds of conflict are there. If you bring home a new car or put an addition on your house, you make yourself a target. You're the neighbor who has more." The consultant sees the present hostility as an outburst of an ageless battle between the haves and the have-nots. He wonders if there would be less anger if the black business community had realized earlier that they have social responsibilities toward their community. For years, he said, many black businesses took from the community without giving anything back.

"A black manager operates in both the First and Third Worlds," said the community development manager for Coca-Cola in Johannesburg. "Faced with the current turmoil, the black manager doesn't know what to do or say. He's trained to be analytical and to reason. But the Third World feels things a lot more. In the current political situation, the youth don't like my model. Anything I say now, they say, 'Shut up. What do you know? Coca-Cola pays your salary.' We are talking two different languages at the moment."

Wars are waged on many different battlefields.

28

Beyers Naude is a man who has given his life to the battle for peace. Naude was nurtured at the heart of the

Afrikaans culture. He sprang from the center of the citadel. His father was the first Dutch Reform pastor to speak the Afrikaans language from a South African pulpit.

Naude's commitment to truth brought him to a place of confrontation with his own culture. In forming the Christian Institute, an interracial, interdenominational organization, he lost his pulpit in the Dutch Reform Church. "You ask me to choose between the church and the Institute," he said. "The real choice is between the church and my soul."

Naude has endured years of banning for the journey he has made. He knows the high price one can pay for following the path to a real peace.

Beyers Naude loves his country passionately. He celebrates his culture deeply. Naude recently spoke of the road he believes South Africa must walk. Referring to his country's white supremacy system, he said, "Such a system cannot be reformed; it must be removed, and if it refuses to be removed it has to be destroyed."

For Beyers Naude, the son of Afrikaners, the need for justice has outstripped the desire for a strong fortress.

29

Years ago, I attended a multiracial ecumenical meeting at a study center on the outskirts of Johannesburg. Our midmorning session was interrupted by a sharp cry: "Fire!"

We rushed out of the building. A section of the brush, close to our quarters, was being devoured by hungry flames.

We had no easy access to water. Fire-fighting equipment was not a part of the center's budget. We quickly grabbed all available shovels and started encircling the conflagration with a trench. It was back-breaking work, but we energized each other. We all knew the destructive potential of the flames if they broke through our defenses.

"No doubt the special branch is up to its old tricks," said the man next to me with a wry smile.

"Surely the South African government would not stoop so low," I protested. "Fire can be a very destructive force. This entire area could have gone up in flames, without our mutual effort."

"Desperate people are capable of desperate acts. They know that if we are out fighting a fire, we can't be in dreaming up new and just structures for our society."

Hours later, we completed the trench. Gasoline was quickly poured into its furrow. A ring of fire swiftly encircled the flaming area. The emergency was over: fire had contained fire.

The area before us lay stripped of all signs of life. It takes a special grace for fire to burn without consuming.

I wished we had had water. Water is softer.

Postscript

When a house is destroyed, a new structure must rise in the empty space, lest the land fall into disrepair. To break down the old is easier than to build the new. One needs a strong foundation to build a home that will endure. One needs a deep and true vision of the task in order to bring the project to fruition.

Where do we find the visions that provide the energy to build a society?

My father lay dying. Suddenly he looked up at me. "I had it! Judy, for one moment I saw it all!"

"What did you see, Dad?"

"I saw why we are here. We are here for no other reason than to show each other how infinitely precious we really are."

In the clarity of our dying, we can discover the deep meaning of our living.

A house whose structure rises from a foundation of justice that springs from love is a house that will endure.

On December 28, 1985, Molly Blackburn, a fifty-five-year-old middle-class white South African, was killed instantly in a head-on car collision.

Mrs. Blackburn was returning home from a visit to a black township. She had been interviewing the parents of black children who had been detained by the police during recent unrest. It had been a typical day for Molly, who had been arrested several times in the past for entering black townships illegally.

This mother of seven had been working relentlessly for years for the freedom and rights of South Africa's black majority. Her demands for justice for all South Africans seemed natural to Molly. It was the only way to bring South Africa home to the place of her peace.

Molly's life was given to a land whose people were exiles on their own soil. The seeds of hate and fear had burrowed deep into people's hearts. The inevitable harvest had come in a spiraling violence that set white against black, black against white, black against black and white against white.

In the midst of this dark and troubled time, Molly dared to live with hope. Driven by a love she experienced as God's love for all of God's children, she acted without fear. There were many times when Molly Blackburn was the only white person present at a mass funeral rally for blacks killed in the racial unrest.

Over ten thousand black and white South Africans gathered together for the memorial service held to celebrate Molly's life. Those present had never before seen such a large, emotional tribute paid to one person.

Members of the multiracial congregation were moved to tears by the eulogy delivered by Dr. Allan Boesak. Dr. Boesak, a Dutch Reform minister as well as an anti-apartheid activist, said of Molly Blackburn, "Few white people have earned so much respect and love among our black people as Molly Blackburn did. We hope and pray another Molly Blackburn will rise; if not, then I don't know what we are trying to build together.

"Molly continued in death doing what she did all her life—bringing us together. This is what this country can and should be. This is what we are fighting for."